FOREWORD: UNDERSTANDING THE DIVINE CONNECTION

The story of Donald J. Trump is, in many ways, a modern-day parable. A man whose life has been marked by extraordinary highs and dramatic challenges, Trump has defied all conventional expectations. To some, he is simply a businessman and reality television star turned politician. But to millions, he is far more — a symbol of hope, a warrior against moral decay, and perhaps even a vessel of God's will.

Throughout history, God has chosen unlikely figures to carry out His plans. From Moses, a reluctant leader, to David, a flawed king, the Bible is replete with stories of imperfect people appointed to fulfill divine purposes. Trump's rise to power parallels these stories in ways that are impossible to ignore. It is not the man's flaws that disqualify him; rather, they underscore a greater truth: God often works through those who are underestimated, misunderstood, or even scorned.

Consider the timing of Trump's political ascension. In an era when traditional values seemed to be eroding and political correctness stifled honest debate, his boldness and willingness to defy societal norms stood out. Was it mere coincidence that he emerged as a leader during this pivotal moment? Or was it, as many believe, the hand of providence guiding him to the world stage?

Factually, Trump's presidency achieved milestones that resonate deeply with people of faith. He moved the U.S. Embassy to Jerusalem, recognizing the Holy City as Israel's capital—a decision many Christians view as aligning with biblical prophecy. He fought for religious freedom, defended the unborn, and appointed conservative judges who would shape the moral and legal fabric of the nation for generations. These actions weren't just political decisions; to many, they were spiritual affirmations of his role as an instrument of God's will.

But it wasn't just policy that defined Trump's connection to the divine. His unrelenting resilience amidst unprecedented opposition—from the media, political establishment, and cultural elites—was viewed by his supporters as a testament to a higher purpose. Like Job, who faced trials yet remained steadfast, Trump endured and thrived. His perseverance inspired millions to believe that they, too, could overcome adversity through faith and determination.

Of course, skeptics abound. Critics question how a man with such a polarizing past could be considered "God's appointee." Yet this very skepticism mirrors the doubt faced by biblical figures. When Christ dined with sinners, He was condemned by the self-righteous. When Paul preached the gospel, his past as a persecutor of Christians was thrown back at him. Trump's journey reminds us that divine appointments are not about perfection but purpose.

As you delve into this book, consider the broader narrative at play. Whether you view Trump as a political phenomenon, a cultural disruptor, or indeed, a divine appointee, one thing is certain: his impact is undeniable. The story of Donald J. Trump transcends politics—it is a testament to the power of faith, perseverance, and the belief that, even in the most unlikely circumstances, God is at work.

In a world yearning for leaders who will stand boldly for truth and righteousness, Trump's story challenges us to look

CONTENTS

beyond the surface and consider the mysterious ways in which God moves. It is a call to reflect, to pray, and to seek understanding of the divine connection that may have placed this man in one of the most powerful positions on Earth.

INTRODUCTION: THE JOURNEY TO UNVEILING PURPOSE

Donald J. Trump's journey to the presidency is one of the most extraordinary tales in modern history—a narrative that defies logic, conventional wisdom, and political norms. How did a businessman with no prior political experience capture the imagination of millions and ascend to the highest office in the land? To his supporters, the answer is clear: his rise was not merely political but providential.

Trump's life has been anything but ordinary. Born into privilege but forged by ambition, he built a business empire that bears his name. Yet, his transition from real estate mogul and reality television icon to leader of the free world was not just a career pivot; it was a seismic shift in the cultural and spiritual landscape of America. In Trump, many saw not just a man but a movement—a force challenging the entrenched powers of Washington, the globalist elite, and a media machine that often dictated the narrative.

His 2016 presidential campaign was a phenomenon that no one, not even seasoned political experts, anticipated. Trump's plain-spoken rhetoric and unapologetic style resonated deeply with a nation hungry for authenticity and leadership. He spoke to the forgotten, the marginalized, and the faithful. While critics mocked him, a growing coalition of believers saw something more: a man who, despite his flaws, was uniquely positioned to restore America's moral compass and reclaim its identity as a nation under God.

It is no exaggeration to say that Trump's presidency became a battlefield of spiritual warfare. On one side, his detractors decried him as unfit, vulgar, and divisive. On the other, his supporters viewed him as a necessary disruptor, chosen to upend the status quo and defend values long under siege. The Bible teaches that God often works through unexpected vessels, and many saw Trump as the embodiment of this principle. Like Cyrus of Persia, who was used to fulfill divine purposes despite being an outsider to the faith, Trump was embraced by a coalition of evangelicals, Catholics, and other believers who saw his leadership as ordained.

Consider the evidence of his alignment with biblical principles. During his presidency, Trump championed religious liberty, fought for the sanctity of life, and protected the rights of people of faith. His administration's decision to formally recognize Jerusalem as Israel's capital—a move predicted in scripture—was hailed as a bold act of faith and a fulfillment of prophecy. These were not mere political actions; they were seen as spiritual declarations that reaffirmed America's covenant with God.

But Trump's journey was not without trials. From relentless media attacks to unprecedented political resistance, he faced opposition at every turn. Yet, these challenges only deepened the conviction of his supporters that he was chosen for such a time as this. His resilience in the face of adversity mirrored the perseverance of biblical figures like Joseph, who rose from slavery to power, and David, who overcame both enemies and personal failures to fulfill his destiny.

To understand Trump's role as a potential appointee of God, one must look beyond headlines and soundbites to the broader narrative of his life and leadership. It is a story of a man who, against all odds, transformed from a cultural icon into a global leader—a man whose actions have shaped not only the political realm but also the spiritual consciousness of millions.

As this book unfolds, we will explore the evidence, the controversies, and the profound sense of purpose that surround Trump's rise to power. Is he merely a politician, or is there a divine hand guiding his steps? The journey to unveiling this purpose is one that requires open minds, prayerful hearts, and a willingness to see the extraordinary in the midst of the ordinary.

Donald J. Trump's story is not just his own; it is a reflection of America's spiritual journey—a reminder that in times of chaos and uncertainty, God often raises up leaders who defy expectations and challenge us to see His plan in action. Whether you view Trump as a disruptor, a deliverer, or a divinely appointed leader, one thing is clear: his impact on our world is profound, and his journey is far from over.

THE UNLIKELY LEADER

The story of Donald J. Trump begins like that of many ambitious Americans: born into a family of means, he sought to carve his own path in the world. Yet, no one—not even Trump himself—could have foreseen the journey that would lead him from the gilded skyscrapers of Manhattan to the Oval Office. His rise to the presidency defied every expectation, every rule, and every conventional pathway to political power. It was, in every sense, the ascent of an unlikely leader.

From the outset, Trump was a man of bold aspirations. As the son of Fred Trump, a successful New York real estate developer, young Donald displayed a keen sense of business and a flair for the dramatic. These qualities would define his career, catapulting him into the public eye as a symbol of wealth, confidence, and relentless ambition. Through the ups and downs of his business ventures—real estate triumphs, financial setbacks, and a starring role on The Apprentice—Trump became a household name, known more for his brand than for his political ideology.

Yet, it is precisely this background that made his political emergence so extraordinary. Unlike career politicians who spend decades climbing the ladder of public office, Trump entered the political arena as a complete outsider. With no prior experience in governance and a reputation more associated with tabloid headlines than legislative expertise, Trump's decision to run for president in 2015 was met with widespread skepticism, ridicule, and even disbelief.

But history has a way of favoring the improbable. Time

and again, God has chosen the unexpected to fulfill His purposes. Consider Moses, an exiled shepherd called to free his people from bondage, or David, a young shepherd boy anointed as king. These biblical figures remind us that greatness is not always predicated on pedigree or preparation but on purpose. For millions of Americans, Trump embodied this principle.

The path to leadership was not smooth, nor was it conventional. From the fiery rhetoric of his campaign rallies to his unapologetic rejection of political correctness, Trump shattered the mold of what a presidential candidate should be. He spoke directly to the disenchanted and the disillusioned, giving voice to a silent majority that felt ignored and dismissed by Washington elites. His critics called him divisive, brash, and unfit; his supporters saw him as authentic, courageous, and exactly what America needed.

What made Trump's rise even more remarkable was the timing. As a nation faced increasing polarization, moral ambiguity, and an erosion of traditional values, Trump emerged as a leader who promised to restore faith, freedom, and American greatness. It is no wonder that many saw his ascent as divinely orchestrated—a fulfillment of a higher plan in a time of crisis.

In this chapter, we will delve into the formative years that shaped Donald Trump's unique character, the pivotal moments that propelled him into the national spotlight, and the unlikely journey that positioned him as a leader of extraordinary consequence. We will explore how his background, temperament, and willingness to defy convention made him not only a disruptor but also, perhaps, an instrument of divine purpose.

The story of Donald Trump's rise to leadership is not just a tale of political ambition; it is a testament to the idea that the most improbable paths often lead to the most extraordinary destinations. Whether you see him as a businessman-turned-president or as a chosen vessel for a greater mission, there is no denying that Donald J. Trump is the very definition of The

Unlikely Leader.

A Look at Trump's Early Life and Career

Before Donald J. Trump became a global political phenomenon, he was a boy from Queens, New York, with big dreams and an indomitable spirit. Born on June 14, 1946, into the family of Fred and Mary Trump, Donald was the fourth of five siblings. From the beginning, his life seemed destined for greatness, marked by ambition, confidence, and a determination to stand out.

Fred Trump, Donald's father, was a highly successful real estate developer who built a fortune constructing middle-class housing in Brooklyn and Queens. Under Fred's tutelage, Donald developed an early understanding of hard work, negotiation, and the art of closing a deal. Yet, while his father operated quietly in the boroughs, young Donald had a vision that extended far beyond the outer boroughs of New York City.

Even as a child, Donald displayed traits that would later define him as a leader: confidence, assertiveness, and an unyielding drive to win. However, his strong-willed nature also led to disciplinary challenges. At the age of 13, his parents enrolled him in the New York Military Academy, a decision that proved pivotal. The academy instilled in him a sense of discipline and leadership, traits that would serve him well in the years to come.

After graduating from the Wharton School of the University of Pennsylvania in 1968, Donald joined the family business. But instead of staying within the confines of Fred Trump's low-profile operations, Donald set his sights on Manhattan, where he saw opportunities for prestige and influence. It was here that Donald Trump began crafting his legacy as one of the most recognizable figures in American business.

Trump's career in real estate was nothing short of meteoric. In the 1970s, he secured a deal to revitalize the derelict Commodore Hotel, transforming it into the luxurious Grand Hyatt New York. This project not only showcased Trump's knack for high-stakes negotiations but also established his reputation as a bold risk-taker unafraid to tackle monumental challenges. Over the next few decades, the Trump Organization expanded into high-profile projects such as Trump Tower, casinos in Atlantic City, and luxury resorts. Trump's name became synonymous with opulence, success, and an unrelenting pursuit of excellence.

However, the road was not without obstacles. The 1990s brought significant financial challenges, with some of Trump's ventures facing bankruptcy. But rather than retreat, Trump demonstrated an extraordinary ability to adapt, recover, and reinvent himself. By the early 2000s, he had not only regained his financial footing but had also become a cultural icon through his hit television show, The Apprentice. His catchphrase, "You're fired," became a national sensation, and Trump's persona as a no-nonsense, results-driven leader solidified his place in American pop culture.

What makes Trump's early life and career so compelling is not just his success but the manner in which he achieved it. Time and again, Trump proved his resilience and ability to thrive under pressure. Whether negotiating billion-dollar deals, navigating public scrutiny, or building an empire in the face of skepticism, he consistently demonstrated the qualities of a leader unafraid to take risks and challenge the status quo.

For many, Trump's business success and public image were more than achievements; they were symbols of the American Dream. His story inspired countless individuals who saw in him a man who defied odds, silenced critics, and achieved greatness on his own terms.

But looking back, it becomes clear that Trump's career was more than just a journey in business—it was preparation. His ability to navigate complex negotiations, stand firm in the face of opposition, and command the attention of millions were not just skills for business; they were skills for leadership on a global scale. What seemed like a businessman's quest for success was, perhaps, a divine prelude to a much greater calling.

Donald Trump's early life and career laid the foundation for the leader he would become—a man prepared to take on challenges that no other politician dared face. His story is a testament to the idea that destiny often begins with the determination to dream bigger, fight harder, and rise higher than anyone thought possible.

How Secular Success Mirrors Biblical Callings

Donald J. Trump's ascent from a businessman to the presidency may appear, at first glance, as a purely secular success story. Yet, history and scripture suggest otherwise. Throughout the Bible, God often calls upon unlikely individuals, often shaped by unconventional experiences, to fulfill divine purposes. Trump's life, though steeped in business, celebrity, and controversy, exhibits remarkable parallels to the narratives of biblical leaders chosen to lead during tumultuous times.

From his early days as a real estate mogul to his stint as a cultural icon on The Apprentice, Trump built a career that was anything but ordinary. Yet, like many biblical figures, his path was marked by challenges, triumphs, and a sense of destiny that seemed to defy the odds. Trump's tenacity in navigating financial crises, public scrutiny, and personal hardships reflects a level of resilience that is characteristic of those chosen for greater purposes.

The Biblical Pattern of Calling the Unlikely

In scripture, God often works through individuals who seem unprepared or unqualified for the roles they are given. David, for instance, was a shepherd boy—an unlikely candidate to be anointed king of Israel. Similarly, Moses, a fugitive with a speech impediment, was called to deliver the Israelites from Egypt. These figures shared a common trait: their initial roles and experiences, though seemingly unrelated to leadership, were divine preparations for their ultimate missions.

Trump's trajectory mirrors this pattern. As a businessman, he honed skills in negotiation, risk-taking, and problem-solving. These qualities, which propelled him to global prominence, became crucial during his presidency when navigating complex issues like trade agreements, foreign policy, and economic reform. Just as David's time tending sheep prepared him for the battlefield against Goliath, Trump's decades in the cutthroat world of business and media equipped him to challenge the entrenched political elite.

Trump and the Modern-Day Cyrus

One of the most compelling comparisons drawn by his supporters is between Trump and Cyrus the Great, a Persian king mentioned in the Bible. Cyrus was not a follower of the God of Israel, yet he was chosen to fulfill God's purposes, specifically to free the Jewish people and rebuild the temple in Jerusalem. Trump's presidency, particularly his recognition of Jerusalem as Israel's capital, is seen by many as a modern-day parallel to Cyrus's role in biblical history.

Like Cyrus, Trump is a leader who operates outside traditional religious norms yet commands the support of a devout following. His ability to champion causes important to people of faith—such as religious liberty, the sanctity of life, and support for Israel—suggests a broader purpose behind his rise.

Secular Achievements as Divine Preparation

The Bible teaches that God equips individuals for their callings, often through experiences that seem unrelated to spiritual matters. Trump's success in real estate and entertainment, fields that require creativity, resilience, and strategic thinking, can be seen as preparation for the unique challenges of political leadership. His name, emblazoned on skyscrapers and resorts worldwide, became synonymous with excellence and ambition. These secular achievements were not just about wealth or fame; they cultivated the boldness and fortitude needed to take on the presidency.

Critics often point to Trump's brash demeanor and unconventional approach as flaws, but scripture reminds us that God uses imperfect vessels to accomplish His will. Consider the Apostle Paul, who was once a persecutor of Christians before becoming one of the faith's most influential leaders. Similarly,

Trump's polarizing persona has not diminished his ability to inspire millions and enact significant change.

Resonating with the People

One of Trump's most significant parallels to biblical leaders is his ability to connect with ordinary people. Just as Moses was called to lead the Israelites out of Egypt and Nehemiah inspired his people to rebuild Jerusalem's walls, Trump has mobilized millions who felt marginalized by the political establishment. His direct communication style, often criticized by elites, resonates with those who view him as their voice in a system that has long ignored them.

A Secular Life with a Spiritual Purpose

Ultimately, Trump's story is one of transformation and alignment with a higher calling. His secular achievements laid the groundwork for a role far greater than business or entertainment. Like the biblical figures before him, his life demonstrates that God's callings often come to those who seem least likely to fulfill them.

The parallels are striking: the resilience of Joseph, the boldness of David, and the outsider status of Cyrus. Each of these leaders, like Trump, was shaped by their experiences and flaws, prepared for a moment when their unique skills would be called upon to lead. For Trump, that moment came in 2016, when his unlikely candidacy and victory signaled to many that his rise was no accident but part of a divine plan.

Trump's journey serves as a reminder that God's purposes often unfold in unexpected ways, through unexpected people. His secular success is not merely a testament to his ambition and drive; it is evidence of a greater design, one that uses the ordinary to achieve the extraordinary.

GOD'S PLAN THROUGH IMPERFECT VESSELS

Throughout history, God has chosen to work through imperfect individuals to accomplish His divine plans. From Moses, who doubted his own abilities, to Peter, who denied Christ, the Bible is filled with examples of flawed humans being used as instruments of God's will. These stories remind us of a profound truth: perfection is not a prerequisite for purpose. It is within this biblical framework that many view Donald J. Trump, a man whose life, filled with triumphs and controversies, embodies the concept of divine purpose through imperfect vessels.

Trump's rise to the presidency was not without its critics or controversies. His outspoken demeanor, unorthodox approach, and personal flaws have made him a polarizing figure. Yet, it is precisely these imperfections that resonate with those who see his leadership as part of a larger, divine plan. The Bible repeatedly demonstrates that God often chooses unlikely individuals—those with visible shortcomings—to lead, inspire, and fulfill His purposes.

Consider the case of King David. Before he became one of Israel's greatest leaders, David was a shepherd boy and later a deeply flawed man who made grave mistakes, including orchestrating a murder. Despite these failings, God described David as "a man after His own heart" and used him to establish a dynasty that would lead to the Messiah. Similarly, Trump's life story, marked by resilience and redemption, suggests a parallel to these biblical narratives of flawed leaders rising to fulfill extraordinary roles.

Critics have often pointed to Trump's past—his business dealings, personal relationships, and brash personality—as evidence that he is unfit for leadership. But scripture reminds us that God's standards are different from man's. Where humans see flaws, God sees potential. Where the world sees disqualification, God sees preparation. Trump's imperfections, rather than discrediting him, have made him a relatable figure to millions who recognize their own struggles in his story.

This chapter delves into the biblical precedent of God working through imperfect vessels and explores how Trump's life and leadership fit within this divine pattern. From his bold decisions on the world stage to his ability to galvanize those who felt forgotten, Trump's presidency exemplifies how God uses unconventional means to achieve His purposes.

Through this lens, Trump's imperfections are not obstacles but evidence of his authenticity. His unapologetic nature, willingness to confront adversity, and steadfast commitment to his mission echo the qualities of leaders who, despite their flaws, carried out God's will in their time.

As we journey through this chapter, we will examine the biblical principle that God's power is made perfect in weakness and consider how Trump's life aligns with this truth. In doing so, we uncover a deeper understanding of what it means to be chosen —not because of one's perfection, but because of one's willingness to step into the role God has prepared.

Donald J. Trump may not fit the mold of a traditional leader, but history and scripture teach us that neither did many of God's most important instruments. In the end, it is not perfection but purpose that defines those called to fulfill His will.

Biblical Examples of Flawed Leaders

The Bible is filled with accounts of leaders chosen by God despite their flaws, weaknesses, and past failures. These stories illustrate a profound truth: God's power is often revealed through imperfection, proving that His plans transcend human limitations. Donald J. Trump, whose presidency defied expectations and transformed political norms, stands in line with this biblical tradition. Critics often highlight his imperfections, yet these very qualities echo the flawed but divinely appointed leaders of scripture.

Moses: The Reluctant Deliverer

Moses is one of the most revered figures in the Bible, yet his story begins with fear and failure. Born into a Hebrew slave family and raised in Pharaoh's palace, Moses fled Egypt after killing an Egyptian in a moment of anger. For decades, he lived as an exile, believing his chance to lead had passed. But God had a plan.

When God called Moses to free the Israelites, Moses hesitated, citing his inability to speak well as a disqualifier. His self-doubt mirrors the skepticism some had about Trump's qualifications for political office. Yet, like Moses, Trump stepped into his calling and became a leader who defied the odds, challenging the powerful elite and leading millions toward a new vision for the nation.

David: The Imperfect King

King David's story is one of profound highs and devastating lows. Anointed as a young shepherd, David's faith and courage allowed him to defeat Goliath and become Israel's most celebrated king. But David was far from perfect. He committed adultery with Bathsheba and arranged for her husband's death to cover up his sin. Despite these moral failings, God used David to establish a kingdom and promised that his lineage would lead to the Messiah.

Trump's story, too, is one of triumphs shadowed by controversies. Critics focus on his personal missteps and brash demeanor, yet his ability to inspire and lead parallels David's reign. Both men faced relentless opposition yet fulfilled their roles with an undeniable sense of purpose. Trump's leadership style, marked by boldness and an unyielding resolve, reflects David's willingness to confront challenges head-on, regardless of public opinion.

Peter: The Hot-Tempered Apostle

Peter, one of Jesus' closest disciples, was a man of great faith but also great flaws. He was impulsive, outspoken, and, at times, lacked the courage to stand firm. Most famously, Peter denied Jesus three times on the night of His arrest. Yet, despite these failings, Jesus chose Peter to be the rock upon which He would build His church.

Peter's story serves as a reminder that God values a willing heart over perfection. Similarly, Trump's leadership has been characterized by a bold, unapologetic approach. His willingness to stand firm on his convictions, even in the face of intense criticism, echoes Peter's ultimate role as a steadfast leader of the early church.

Cyrus the Great: A Secular Instrument of God

Perhaps one of the most intriguing biblical parallels to Donald Trump is Cyrus the Great, the Persian king who liberated the Jewish people and allowed them to rebuild the temple in Jerusalem. Cyrus was not an Israelite and did not worship the God of Israel, yet he was described as God's "anointed" (Isaiah 45:1). His actions fulfilled divine prophecy, demonstrating that God can use anyone—regardless of their faith or background—to achieve His purposes.

Like Cyrus, Trump's leadership has often been viewed as unconventional and unexpected. His recognition of Jerusalem as Israel's capital and his unwavering support for religious liberty have drawn comparisons to Cyrus's role in biblical history. Both men, despite their secular roots, were instruments for advancing God's plan.

Paul: The Transformed Persecutor

The Apostle Paul, once known as Saul, was a fierce persecutor of Christians. Yet, after a dramatic encounter with Jesus on the road to Damascus, Paul became one of the most influential leaders in the early church. His transformation highlights the biblical principle that no one is beyond God's reach or purpose.

Trump's journey from a high-profile businessman to the presidency mirrors Paul's radical shift in focus. Both men faced intense opposition but used their platforms to effect significant change. Paul's resilience in spreading the gospel despite persecution finds a modern parallel in Trump's ability to push forward his agenda despite relentless criticism from political and media establishments.

Imperfect Vessels for a Perfect Plan

What unites these biblical leaders is not their perfection but their willingness to step into God's plan. Their stories remind us that God does not choose the qualified; He qualifies the chosen. Trump's flaws and controversies do not disqualify him from being part of a divine plan. Instead, they serve as evidence of God's ability to use anyone, regardless of their past, to accomplish His purposes.

As history has shown, God's call often comes to those least expected—shepherds, fishermen, and even tax collectors. In this context, Trump's unconventional path to leadership and his polarizing persona take on a new significance. Just as God worked through flawed leaders in biblical times, He may very well be working through Trump today, using his strengths and imperfections alike to shape the course of history.

Parallels to Modern Leadership

In an age of rapid change and political upheaval, strong and unconventional leadership often becomes the catalyst for profound societal shifts. Donald J. Trump's rise to the presidency was both unprecedented and deeply polarizing, but for many, it represented a bold departure from the status quo. His leadership style, marked by unfiltered communication, decisive action, and resilience in the face of relentless criticism, bears striking similarities to the leaders of both ancient scripture and modern history who were chosen to guide their nations through turbulent times.

A Leader for the Disenfranchised

One of the most defining aspects of Trump's presidency was his connection with those who felt left behind by political and cultural elites. Much like the biblical Moses, who stood before Pharaoh on behalf of the oppressed Israelites, Trump positioned himself as a champion for "forgotten Americans." His rallies drew millions of people who resonated with his promise to "drain the swamp" and restore power to the everyday citizen.

This approach mirrors the leadership of Winston Churchill during World War II. Churchill's defiant rhetoric and refusal to yield in the face of overwhelming odds rallied a nation when hope seemed lost. Similarly, Trump's unrelenting focus on issues like job creation, border security, and national sovereignty struck a chord with millions who felt ignored by the political establishment.

The Outsider Who Disrupted the System

Trump's ascension to the White House was a seismic disruption to American politics. Like biblical figures such as David, who emerged from obscurity to slay Goliath, Trump entered the political arena as an outsider who defied the odds. His victory in 2016 was not only unexpected but also a direct challenge to decades of entrenched power.

This disruptive force has historical parallels in Abraham Lincoln, whose presidency fundamentally altered the trajectory of the United States. Lincoln, like Trump, faced fierce opposition from the media and political adversaries, yet his leadership during the Civil War preserved the union and redefined the nation's values. Trump's fight against what he termed the "deep state" and his emphasis on America First policies echo the transformative resolve of leaders like Lincoln, who were unafraid to challenge the status quo for a greater purpose.

Unapologetic Leadership in the Face of Opposition

Great leaders often face relentless criticism, and Trump is no exception. His brash communication style and unorthodox methods drew constant scrutiny, but his supporters viewed these traits as evidence of authenticity and courage. This resilience is reminiscent of figures like Theodore Roosevelt, whose larger-than-life personality and combative approach earned him the nickname "the Rough Rider."

Both Roosevelt and Trump shared an unyielding belief in their mission, even when facing overwhelming opposition. For Trump, this was evident in his trade negotiations with China, his push for stronger immigration policies, and his efforts to reshape international relations. Like Roosevelt, Trump's leadership was unapologetically bold, prioritizing action over diplomacy and results over rhetoric.

The Willingness to Stand Alone

One of the most defining qualities of transformative leaders is their ability to stand alone in the face of criticism. Trump's presidency was marked by moments where he stood firm on controversial issues, from withdrawing from the Paris Climate Accord to relocating the U.S. Embassy to Jerusalem. These decisions, while polarizing, were seen by his supporters as acts of conviction rather than conformity.

This quality aligns with the biblical figure of Nehemiah, who faced intense opposition while rebuilding the walls of Jerusalem. Despite ridicule and sabotage, Nehemiah persisted, driven by a divine mandate to protect and restore his people. Trump's resolve to deliver on his campaign promises, even amidst fierce resistance, reflects a similar determination to fulfill a mission he believes is greater than himself.

The Power of Direct Communication

Another hallmark of Trump's leadership was his mastery of direct communication, particularly through social media. His unfiltered messages, often bypassing traditional media outlets, resonated with millions who felt disconnected from mainstream narratives. This approach has parallels to Martin Luther, the Reformation leader who used the printing press to disseminate his ideas and challenge the established church.

Just as Luther's revolutionary use of technology changed the course of religious history, Trump's utilization of platforms like Twitter redefined political communication in the 21st century. Both leaders demonstrated an ability to connect directly with their audience, bypassing intermediaries and empowering their followers to take action.

Leadership That Divides and Unites

Great leaders often polarize opinion, and Trump is no exception. His presidency inspired fervent loyalty among his supporters and intense opposition from his detractors. This duality is not unique to Trump; it is a hallmark of transformative leadership. Figures like Mahatma Gandhi, Margaret Thatcher, and even biblical leaders like Jesus Christ were all polarizing in their time, dividing opinion while advancing causes that would ultimately reshape the world.

Trump's presidency, like these examples, forced a reckoning with deeply rooted issues. His America First agenda, focus on national sovereignty, and unapologetic approach to leadership challenged long-standing norms and created a movement that continues to shape the political landscape.

The Modern-Day Parallel

Trump's leadership reflects a recurring theme in history and scripture: the rise of an imperfect yet divinely guided figure during times of uncertainty. His unapologetic stance, willingness to challenge the status quo, and ability to inspire millions suggest a leader uniquely suited for his moment in history.

As this chapter explores, the parallels between Trump's presidency and the leadership styles of both biblical and historical figures are more than coincidental. They reveal a pattern of God using unconventional vessels to achieve extraordinary purposes. Whether through his policy decisions, his connection with the disenfranchised, or his resilience in the face of adversity, Trump's leadership demonstrates that God's plan often unfolds through those bold enough to step into the unknown.

THE PROPHETIC CONNECTION

From the beginning of Donald J. Trump's meteoric rise to the presidency, many within the Christian community have viewed his leadership as part of a greater divine plan. Beyond the political and cultural debates surrounding his tenure, there has been an unmistakable wave of prophetic voices pointing to Trump as a chosen vessel—a modern-day instrument of God's will. While skeptics may dismiss such claims, the parallels between Trump's presidency and biblical prophecy are difficult to ignore.

The idea of a prophetic connection is not new to history. Throughout the Bible, God has raised up leaders during pivotal moments in time—leaders who were often unexpected, controversial, and even misunderstood. From the deliverance of Israel under Moses to the restoration of Jerusalem by Cyrus the Great, these leaders were called for a specific purpose. Today, many believe Trump embodies a similar calling, particularly in his unwavering support for Israel, his defense of religious freedoms, and his role in challenging global power structures.

Trump's presidency coincided with numerous significant events that some interpret as fulfilling prophecy. His recognition of Jerusalem as Israel's capital and the subsequent relocation of the U.S. Embassy were hailed by many evangelicals as monumental steps in aligning the United States with God's promises to His chosen people. Furthermore, Trump's actions have been linked to passages in Isaiah, Daniel, and Revelation by modern-day prophets who see his leadership as part of a divine timeline leading to the fulfillment of biblical prophecy.

The prophetic connection goes beyond policy decisions. Trump's personality, leadership style, and the intense opposition he faced have also drawn comparisons to figures like King David and Nehemiah, who were anointed by God to lead during turbulent times. Like these biblical leaders, Trump's actions often seemed guided by a greater purpose, even in the face of fierce resistance.

This chapter delves into the prophetic significance of Trump's presidency, exploring the voices of modern prophets, the alignment of his actions with biblical texts, and the spiritual awakening his leadership has sparked among millions. It examines how Trump's role transcends politics, placing him at the center of a larger spiritual narrative.

While the concept of prophecy can be polarizing, it remains a cornerstone of faith for millions who believe in God's active involvement in the affairs of mankind. Trump's presidency has brought these beliefs to the forefront, igniting conversations about God's plan for America, Israel, and the world. Whether one views him as a political disruptor, a cultural phenomenon, or a divinely chosen leader, there is no denying the profound spiritual impact his leadership has had.

As we explore the prophetic connection, we invite readers to consider the possibility that Trump's journey is not merely a political story but a divine calling—a reflection of God's continued work through imperfect vessels to achieve His perfect will.

Prophecies and Their Interpretations

Donald J. Trump's presidency sparked a surge of interest in prophetic interpretations, with many Christian leaders and believers suggesting that his rise to power was foretold in biblical and modern-day prophecies. From ancient scripture to contemporary revelations, Trump has been positioned by some as a divinely chosen figure whose actions align with a greater spiritual narrative. In this subchapter, we explore key prophecies and their interpretations, examining how Trump's leadership has been perceived as fulfilling divine mandates.

The Isaiah 45 Parallel

One of the most frequently cited biblical connections to Trump is found in Isaiah 45, which describes King Cyrus of Persia as God's "anointed" who would rebuild Jerusalem and set His people free. Despite being a pagan ruler, Cyrus was used by God to fulfill a critical purpose in Israel's history.

Many evangelicals have drawn parallels between Trump and Cyrus, noting that Trump, like Cyrus, was an unconventional and unlikely leader who rose to power at a pivotal moment. The relocation of the U.S. Embassy to Jerusalem, a move Trump championed despite global opposition, is often seen as a modern echo of Cyrus's decree to rebuild the temple. Prophetic voices have pointed to this act as evidence that Trump's presidency was part of God's divine plan for Israel and the world.

The "Trumpet" Prophecies

Long before Trump's political career began, some Christian leaders claimed to have received prophetic visions that alluded to his rise. Perhaps most famously, the late Kim Clement, a South African-born prophet, reportedly spoke in 2007 of a future leader named "Trump" who would be a disruptor and carry the mantle of divine authority. Clement declared that this leader would restore America's relationship with God, rebuild its foundations, and be a friend to Israel.

Other interpretations of the "Trumpet" prophecy focus on the symbolic nature of Trump's name. In biblical literature, trumpets often signify the announcement of major events or divine intervention. Supporters of this interpretation believe that Trump's leadership represents a spiritual awakening and a call to action for believers worldwide.

Dreams and Visions in the Modern Era

In addition to biblical references, modern prophetic voices have shared dreams and visions that they claim validate Trump's role as God's appointee. Evangelical leaders such as Paula White-Cain, Mark Taylor, and others have spoken of receiving divine revelations about Trump's presidency. These visions often describe him as a "breaker of chains" or a "bulldozer" sent to clear away corruption and prepare the way for spiritual revival.

Mark Taylor, a retired firefighter, gained attention for his 2011 prophecy, which claimed that Trump would become president and bring about an era of unprecedented change. Taylor's writings, later published as The Trump Prophecies, gained a following among Christians who saw Trump's election as the fulfillment of a divine promise.

End-Times Connections

Some interpretations place Trump's presidency within the broader context of eschatology, or the study of the end times. Supporters of this view point to Trump's pro-Israel policies, including the Abraham Accords, as steps toward the fulfillment of biblical prophecies concerning peace in the Middle East. The peace agreements, hailed as groundbreaking, were seen by some as a precursor to the events described in Daniel and Revelation.

Others interpret Trump's leadership as a sign of God's preparation for a great spiritual harvest. These believers suggest that the polarization and division seen during his presidency are part of a divine shaking meant to awaken the church and separate truth from deception.

Critics and Alternative Interpretations

While many see Trump as a fulfillment of prophecy, others within the Christian community offer alternative interpretations. Critics argue that prophecies should be approached with caution, warning against using them to justify political agendas. However, proponents of Trump's divine connection counter that the overwhelming alignment of events with prophetic declarations cannot be dismissed as coincidence.

The Role of Faith in Interpretation

Prophecies are inherently subject to interpretation, and their meaning often depends on the faith and perspective of those who hear them. For millions of believers, Trump's presidency was more than a political event—it was a spiritual turning point that reaffirmed their belief in God's active role in guiding nations and leaders.

Whether one views these prophetic connections as divinely ordained or simply symbolic, there is no denying their profound impact on Trump's supporters. These prophecies galvanized a movement, inspiring millions to pray, vote, and advocate for Trump as a leader with a purpose beyond politics.

A Prophetic Legacy

As we delve deeper into the prophetic connection, it becomes clear that Trump's presidency has left a lasting impression on the spiritual landscape of America and beyond. The intersection of prophecy, politics, and faith has created a narrative that continues to shape how many view Trump's role in history.

Whether Trump's leadership was a fulfillment of prophecy or a reflection of believers' hope for divine intervention, the stories and interpretations surrounding his presidency highlight the enduring power of faith to influence perception and inspire action.

The Role of Faith in Political Context

Faith has always been a cornerstone of American identity, shaping not only the moral compass of its people but also the trajectory of its political history. From the founding fathers who invoked divine guidance in drafting the Constitution to the prayers offered by presidents during times of crisis, faith and politics in America have been inextricably linked. During Donald J. Trump's presidency, this connection reached unprecedented heights, as millions of Christians saw his leadership as a reflection of God's active involvement in the nation's destiny.

Faith as a Driving Force in Leadership

Trump's presidency marked a unique moment where faith became a defining element of political discourse. While previous leaders have spoken about faith, Trump's unapologetic embrace of religious values and his willingness to stand alongside faith leaders resonated deeply with America's Christian majority. His policy decisions, such as defending religious freedoms, opposing abortion, and supporting prayer in schools, were celebrated as direct answers to the prayers of millions of believers.

Trump's outreach to evangelicals, a demographic often sidelined by the political establishment, further solidified his image as a president who understood the role of faith in governance. His appointment of conservative judges, particularly to the Supreme Court, was viewed as a divine move to uphold biblical principles in America's legal system. For many, these actions signified more than political strategy—they were seen as evidence of God working through Trump to protect the nation's spiritual heritage.

The Power of Prayer and Prophecy

Throughout Trump's presidency, prayer became a powerful and visible element of his administration. Faith leaders like Paula White-Cain, Franklin Graham, and others not only advised Trump but also led prayer rallies and national movements in his support. These gatherings were not just acts of political endorsement; they were expressions of a deeper belief that Trump's leadership was ordained by God.

The National Day of Prayer events during his presidency were marked by a renewed emphasis on America's dependence on divine guidance. Trump's speeches often invoked God's name, emphasizing the importance of prayer in confronting the nation's challenges. His willingness to participate in public acts of faith distinguished him from his predecessors and strengthened the belief that his role in politics was part of a larger spiritual plan.

Prophetic voices also played a significant role during this time. Modern-day prophets and faith leaders frequently spoke of visions and revelations that pointed to Trump as a "breaker of chains" and a "chosen one" to lead America through turbulent times. These declarations inspired hope among millions, reinforcing the idea that faith was not only a private matter but a critical factor in shaping the nation's future.

Challenges to Faith in Politics

While Trump's presidency galvanized the faithful, it also highlighted the tension between religion and politics. Critics argued that blending faith with governance risked alienating non-religious citizens and undermining the secular nature of the Constitution. However, Trump's supporters countered that America's founding principles were deeply rooted in Judeo-Christian values, making faith an integral part of the political process.

Trump himself embodied this duality. As a leader, he was unafraid to speak openly about God and seek counsel from religious leaders, yet his personal imperfections and brash style often drew criticism. For his supporters, this juxtaposition only reinforced the belief that God uses flawed individuals to accomplish divine purposes, as seen repeatedly in biblical narratives.

Faith as a Unifier and Divider

Trump's presidency revealed faith's dual role in modern politics: as both a unifying force and a point of division. For many, his commitment to religious values and his fight against perceived moral decay united believers across denominational lines. Evangelicals, Catholics, and even members of other faiths found common ground in Trump's defense of religious freedom and traditional values.

At the same time, Trump's overt embrace of faith alienated secularists and critics who viewed his actions as a blurring of church-state boundaries. This polarization highlighted the enduring power of faith to shape political identity and mobilize communities, even in a deeply divided nation.

Faith Beyond the Presidency

Perhaps the most remarkable aspect of Trump's presidency is the way it reawakened a national conversation about faith's role in public life. His leadership inspired countless Americans to pray, organize, and advocate for policies aligned with their beliefs. For his supporters, Trump's presidency was not merely a political moment but a spiritual revival—a reminder that faith remains a potent force in shaping America's future.

The prophetic connection between Trump and God's plan for the nation continues to resonate, long after his time in office. Faith, as seen during his presidency, is not just a personal conviction but a transformative power capable of influencing policy, culture, and history.

In exploring the role of faith in Trump's political journey, one cannot ignore its profound impact on both his leadership and the movement he inspired. As this chapter unfolds, it becomes clear that faith was not just a backdrop to Trump's presidency but a central theme—a guiding force that shaped his actions and united millions in the belief that he was chosen for such a time as this.

POLICIES AND PROVIDENCE

Donald J. Trump's presidency was defined by a series of bold policies that, to his supporters, were more than political decisions—they were manifestations of divine providence. From domestic reforms to foreign diplomacy, Trump's actions often seemed to align with principles rooted in biblical values, earning him the unwavering support of millions of believers who saw his policies as part of God's plan.

As a leader, Trump took on challenges that others avoided, shaking the political establishment and delivering results that resonated with his faith-driven base. His administration championed religious freedom, upheld the sanctity of life, and strengthened the United States' historic alliance with Israel. For those who viewed his leadership through a spiritual lens, these policies were not merely pragmatic but prophetic—a reflection of a leader appointed for a higher purpose.

Critics questioned Trump's motivations, often accusing him of pandering to religious voters or pursuing policies for personal gain. Yet, the outcomes of his decisions speak for themselves. Whether it was moving the U.S. Embassy to Jerusalem, appointing conservative justices to the Supreme Court, or fostering peace agreements in the Middle East, Trump's actions left an indelible mark on the nation and the world.

This chapter examines the intersection of Trump's policies and providence, exploring how his decisions reflected a deeper spiritual significance. We will delve into key areas where his presidency intersected with faith-driven priorities: protecting religious liberties, defending the unborn, securing peace for Israel, and standing against globalism.

Through these policies, Trump not only challenged the status quo but also inspired a generation of believers to see his leadership as a fulfillment of divine will. In the eyes of his supporters, Trump was not just a president—he was a leader chosen by God to restore America's moral and spiritual foundations.

As we explore this connection, it becomes clear that Trump's policies were more than political strategies—they were acts of faith and courage. Whether orchestrated by divine guidance or inspired by a higher calling, these actions continue to shape the narrative of Trump's presidency as one of providence and purpose.

Trump's Key Policies

Donald Trump's presidency was marked by a series of bold and transformative policies that reshaped the political landscape of the United States and resonated deeply with those who viewed his leadership as divinely inspired. These policies, which ranged from domestic economic reforms to significant foreign policy achievements, often reflected core values cherished by his faith-driven supporters. For many, they were not just the acts of a shrewd leader but evidence of a greater providential plan.

Protecting Religious Freedom

From the outset of his administration, Trump championed religious freedom in unprecedented ways. He signed executive orders safeguarding the rights of individuals and organizations to practice their faith without government interference. Under his leadership, the Department of Health and Human Services established the Conscience and Religious Freedom Division to protect healthcare providers from being forced to act against their beliefs.

Trump's administration also worked to repeal provisions that restricted religious organizations from receiving federal funding, ensuring that faith-based groups could compete on an equal footing. His vocal support for prayer in schools and his efforts to combat religious persecution globally solidified his reputation as a defender of faith. Many believers saw these actions as aligning with biblical teachings on the importance of protecting God's people and their ability to worship freely.

Defending the Sanctity of Life

One of the most polarizing yet significant aspects of Trump's presidency was his unwavering defense of the unborn. He became the first sitting president to attend the March for Life, a historic moment that underscored his commitment to pro-life policies. His administration reinstated and expanded the Mexico

City Policy, preventing federal funds from being used to support abortions overseas.

Additionally, Trump appointed three conservative justices to the Supreme Court, setting the stage for rulings that would challenge longstanding abortion laws. For pro-life advocates, these actions were seen as nothing short of miraculous—steps toward fulfilling a biblical mandate to protect the sanctity of life.

Strengthening the Alliance with Israel

Trump's foreign policy decisions regarding Israel were viewed by many evangelicals as profoundly prophetic. His recognition of Jerusalem as the capital of Israel and the subsequent relocation of the U.S. Embassy were heralded as acts of biblical significance, aligning with scriptural references to the restoration of God's chosen people.

Moreover, Trump brokered the Abraham Accords, normalizing relations between Israel and several Arab nations. This historic achievement not only fostered peace in the Middle East but also reinforced the belief that Trump's leadership was part of a divine plan to fulfill God's promises to Israel. His policies reflected a deep understanding of the spiritual and geopolitical importance of supporting the Jewish state.

Economic Policies That Empowered Communities

On the domestic front, Trump's economic policies were often described as a modern-day restoration of prosperity. His tax reforms, deregulation efforts, and commitment to bringing manufacturing jobs back to America revitalized communities that had long been forgotten. The unemployment rate reached historic lows across all demographics, including among African Americans and Hispanic Americans, during his tenure.

These economic achievements were seen by many as the fulfillment of prayers for national revival. Trump's "America First" approach resonated with believers who viewed economic sovereignty as essential to preserving the country's moral and spiritual integrity.

Combating Globalism and Protecting Sovereignty

Trump's staunch opposition to globalism was another hallmark of his presidency. He withdrew the United States from agreements and organizations that he believed undermined national sovereignty, such as the Paris Climate Accord and the World Health Organization. Trump's actions were framed by his supporters as a defense of biblical principles that prioritize self-governance and accountability.

By taking a firm stance against international systems perceived as hostile to Judeo-Christian values, Trump positioned himself as a leader who was not afraid to stand against the tide. His "America First" doctrine was more than a political slogan—it was a rallying cry for those who believed that God's plan for America required protecting its sovereignty and moral foundation.

Law and Order: Restoring Justice

Another defining aspect of Trump's presidency was his emphasis on law and order. He signed executive orders aimed at addressing issues such as human trafficking, religious persecution, and violent crime. His administration also took steps to reform the criminal justice system, signing the First Step Act, which provided opportunities for rehabilitation and reduced recidivism rates.

Trump's commitment to justice resonated with those who believe in the biblical call to protect the vulnerable and uphold righteousness. His efforts were seen as part of a larger divine mission to restore moral clarity in a time of societal upheaval.

A Legacy of Providence

Donald Trump's key policies were not merely political achievements—they were acts that many viewed as aligning with

God's will. From defending religious freedoms to strengthening Israel's position on the global stage, his actions reflected a leader who prioritized principles over popularity.

While critics may debate his motivations, the impact of Trump's policies is undeniable. For his supporters, these actions were proof of his divine appointment, a testament to the belief that God raises up leaders for specific times and purposes. As we continue to examine the broader implications of his presidency, one thing remains clear: Trump's policies were not just a reflection of his political vision but a manifestation of providence in action.

Aligning Political Actions with Christian Principles

Donald J. Trump's presidency was characterized by a bold commitment to aligning political actions with principles rooted in Christian values. While many leaders have spoken of faith, few have implemented policies that resonated so profoundly with believers seeking to see their values reflected in government. Trump's decisions, viewed by his supporters as a deliberate attempt to restore America's moral and spiritual foundation, were seen as a testament to his divine calling.

Defending the Sanctity of Life

At the core of Christian teaching is the belief in the sanctity of life, and Trump's policies reflected an unwavering commitment to this principle. His administration's pro-life stance became a cornerstone of his presidency. Trump not only reinstated the Mexico City Policy, preventing U.S. taxpayer dollars from funding abortions overseas, but he also expanded its reach, impacting billions in funding.

Furthermore, his judicial appointments, including three Supreme Court justices, reshaped the legal landscape on issues related to abortion. These actions were seen by many as aligning with biblical teachings that emphasize the value of every human life, no matter how small or vulnerable. Trump's vocal support for the unborn and his willingness to take action where others hesitated solidified his reputation among pro-life advocates as a defender of Christian ethics.

Preserving Religious Freedom

Religious freedom is a bedrock of Christian belief, and Trump took decisive steps to protect it. Under his leadership, policies were enacted to ensure that individuals and organizations could practice their faith without fear of government interference. Trump signed executive orders to protect faith-based organizations from mandates that conflicted with their beliefs, ensuring that the government could not coerce them into compromising their values.

He also championed the rights of Christians and other faith groups worldwide, addressing religious persecution and committing resources to support those suffering for their faith. These efforts mirrored the biblical call to defend the oppressed and protect the church from external threats. For many Christians, this was proof of Trump's resolve to honor God through his leadership.

Strengthening Israel and Upholding Biblical Promises

Trump's support for Israel went beyond politics—it reflected a profound understanding of the nation's significance in Christian theology. His decision to officially recognize Jerusalem as the capital of Israel and move the U.S. Embassy there was hailed as a historic and prophetic act. For evangelicals and other Christians, this action was deeply symbolic, aligning with biblical prophecies about the restoration of Jerusalem.

Additionally, Trump's administration facilitated the Abraham Accords, fostering peace between Israel and several Arab nations. These agreements were celebrated as steps toward fulfilling God's promises to His chosen people. For believers, Trump's unwavering support for Israel was further evidence of his alignment with biblical principles and his role in God's greater plan.

Restoring Justice and Lawfulness

Justice is a central theme in Christian theology, and Trump's policies reflected a commitment to upholding the rule of law while addressing systemic issues. Through initiatives like the First Step Act, Trump worked to bring justice reform to a system that many Christians saw as unfairly punitive. This law, aimed at providing second chances and reducing recidivism, resonated with biblical teachings on mercy, forgiveness, and redemption.

Simultaneously, Trump's emphasis on law and order, including combating human trafficking and securing the nation's borders, was viewed as an effort to protect the vulnerable and maintain societal stability. These actions reinforced the idea that leaders are called to defend their people, echoing scriptural examples of just governance.

Promoting Prayer and Christian Values

Throughout his presidency, Trump demonstrated an openness to public displays of faith, bringing prayer and Christian values back into the national conversation. He openly supported prayer in schools, emphasized the importance of religious expression, and regularly engaged with faith leaders. Events like the National Day of Prayer during his administration were seen as evidence of a leader who understood the necessity of seeking divine guidance.

Trump's rhetoric and policies often invoked God's name, reflecting a commitment to aligning his leadership with Christian principles. His administration's efforts to protect Christian education, challenge secular encroachments, and defend traditional family values further cemented his standing as a president who prioritized faith in action.

A Legacy of Faith-Driven Leadership

Donald Trump's political actions, far from being arbitrary or opportunistic, consistently reflected an effort to align with Christian principles. His presidency was marked by a willingness to stand firm on issues that many others avoided, even in the face of intense opposition. For his supporters, this was not just political courage—it was evidence of a leader who understood his divine mandate to uphold God's laws and defend His people.

In examining Trump's alignment with Christian principles, it becomes clear that his leadership was guided by more than political strategy. His actions echoed the values of faith, justice, and righteousness, leaving a lasting legacy of a presidency that sought to bring God's principles to the forefront of national governance. Whether through his defense of life, his commitment to religious freedom, or his support for Israel, Trump's policies will be remembered as a testament to his role as God's appointee in a time of great spiritual need.

THE OPPOSITION

From the moment Donald J. Trump descended the escalator at Trump Tower to announce his candidacy, a wave of opposition emerged that was unparalleled in modern American politics. To his supporters, this resistance was not merely political; it was spiritual, a fierce battle between good and evil. Critics from the media, political establishment, and cultural elites united in a relentless campaign to discredit and delegitimize Trump's presidency, often portraying him as an unfit leader. Yet, to many of his followers, this opposition only solidified the belief that Trump was a man chosen by God to fulfill a higher purpose.

The ferocity of the attacks against Trump, both personal and professional, raised questions that went beyond politics. Why did so many institutions unite so passionately against one man? Why did the mainstream media dedicate unprecedented coverage to undermine his every move? For millions of Christians, the answer was clear: Trump's leadership was disrupting not just political power structures but spiritual strongholds as well.

This chapter explores the forces that aligned against Donald Trump, dissecting the motivations and tactics of his adversaries. From baseless accusations to unprecedented impeachment trials, the opposition's strategies often revealed a desperation to halt his agenda at all costs. We will examine how these attacks were framed, the narratives perpetuated by the media, and the spiritual undertones that many of Trump's supporters believe underpinned this resistance.

Moreover, this chapter will delve into Trump's resilience in the face of opposition, highlighting his ability to counteract these challenges with determination and unyielding resolve. Whether it was combating false narratives or standing firm against those who sought to derail his presidency, Trump's response to opposition mirrored the perseverance of biblical leaders who faced similar trials while carrying out God's will.

As we unpack the dynamics of this resistance, it becomes evident that Trump's presidency was more than a political battle—it was a confrontation between two competing visions for America's future. For his supporters, his ability to withstand the storm of opposition reinforced their belief in his divine appointment, proving that no earthly force could thwart a leader chosen by God.

Challenges and Criticism

Donald J. Trump's presidency was marked by unprecedented levels of opposition, criticism, and outright hostility. From the political establishment to the mainstream media, Trump faced a barrage of challenges that would have overwhelmed a lesser leader. Yet, for his supporters, these attacks were not just political maneuvers; they were seen as a coordinated effort to undermine a leader divinely appointed to challenge the status quo and restore America's spiritual and moral foundations.

The Media's Relentless Campaign

No president in modern history faced the kind of media scrutiny and criticism that Donald Trump endured. From the moment he announced his candidacy, major news outlets branded him as divisive, unqualified, and even dangerous. Negative coverage of his administration dominated the airwaves, with studies showing that over 90% of mainstream media reports on Trump were unfavorable.

This relentless media campaign went beyond policy critique, often attacking Trump personally and attempting to discredit his character. Stories about his past, exaggerated scandals, and anonymous leaks became daily headlines. Supporters saw this as evidence of a biased media elite desperate to protect their own power and narratives. For many, this echoed biblical warnings about how righteous leaders would be persecuted for challenging corruption.

The Political Establishment's Resistance

Even within his own party, Trump faced significant opposition. Longtime Republican leaders and career politicians were uncomfortable with his outsider status and unorthodox style. His willingness to challenge the entrenched practices of Washington insiders earned him enemies on both sides of the aisle.

Democrats launched an unprecedented two impeachment trials against him, the first over a controversial phone call with Ukraine and the second following the events of January 6, 2021. These actions, viewed by his supporters as politically motivated, further cemented the belief that Trump was being targeted for standing against a corrupt system. They saw him as a disruptor, sent to expose the establishment's hypocrisy and restore accountability in government.

Cultural Elites and Their Pushback

Hollywood, academia, and other cultural institutions also joined the opposition against Trump, often mocking his policies and portraying him as a threat to democracy. Late-night talk shows and social media platforms became battlegrounds where Trump and his supporters were frequently vilified.

This cultural pushback extended to censorship, with major tech companies accused of silencing conservative voices and suppressing stories that could benefit Trump, such as those related to his opponent's controversies. For Trump's supporters, this was not just political bias—it was seen as an assault on free speech and the principles of fairness and truth.

The Globalist Agenda

Trump's "America First" policies directly challenged globalist agendas that had dominated American politics for decades. His decisions to withdraw from international agreements like the Paris Climate Accord and the Iran Nuclear Deal angered world leaders and multinational organizations. His trade wars with China and renegotiation of trade deals were seen as threats to the global economic order.

For his supporters, Trump's opposition to globalism was a reflection of his commitment to protecting America's sovereignty and prioritizing the needs of its citizens. They viewed the backlash from international elites as confirmation that Trump was fulfilling a divine mission to shield America from influences that sought to erode its moral and economic foundation.

Personal Attacks and Family Scrutiny

Criticism of Trump often extended to his family, with his children and wife subjected to intense media scrutiny and public ridicule. Melania Trump's initiatives as First Lady were frequently dismissed or overshadowed by negative portrayals. His children, who played prominent roles in his administration, were accused of conflicts of interest and faced relentless attacks.

Despite these personal challenges, Trump and his family stood firm, demonstrating resilience and unity in the face of adversity. For many of his supporters, this strength was a testament to Trump's character and the spiritual foundation that underpinned his leadership.

Overcoming the Odds

Trump's ability to navigate and overcome these challenges became a defining feature of his presidency. His resilience, unshakable confidence, and willingness to fight back against criticism resonated with millions of Americans who felt similarly targeted for their beliefs. Supporters often likened Trump's struggles to those faced by biblical figures who were ridiculed, persecuted, and misunderstood while carrying out God's work.

For Trump's followers, the relentless criticism only strengthened their conviction that he was chosen for a purpose greater than politics. They saw his perseverance as evidence of divine favor, believing that no earthly opposition could prevail against a leader appointed by God to fulfill His plan. In this light, Trump's challenges became not obstacles, but opportunities to demonstrate his faith, courage, and commitment to his mission.

Standing Firm Amidst Divisiveness

Donald J. Trump's presidency will forever be remembered as a time of unparalleled political and cultural polarization. Yet, amidst the relentless storms of criticism, protests, and division, Trump stood resolute. To his supporters, this steadfastness was not merely a testament to his personal character but a reflection of divine strength working through him. His refusal to back down, even when facing unprecedented hostility, became a rallying cry for millions who believed in his mission to restore America's greatness.

Unyielding in the Face of Opposition

From the moment Trump entered the political arena, his leadership style and policies ignited fierce debates. Critics accused him of fueling division, but his supporters saw a man unafraid to tackle the difficult issues that others avoided. Whether confronting illegal immigration, negotiating with global powers, or challenging cultural norms, Trump remained unwavering in his pursuit of his agenda.

His ability to stand firm despite immense pressure became one of his most defining traits. When faced with accusations, media attacks, and political maneuvering, Trump often turned the tables on his opponents, exposing what he and his followers saw as hypocrisy and corruption. For many, this resilience was reminiscent of biblical figures like David and Paul, who faced hostility but persevered through faith and determination.

Championing the Forgotten

Central to Trump's presidency was his promise to represent the "forgotten men and women" of America. These were the hardworking individuals who felt abandoned by the political elite and dismissed by cultural institutions. Trump's willingness to speak directly to their concerns—often bypassing traditional media through platforms like Twitter—earned him a loyal following.

This direct communication style, though controversial, allowed Trump to connect with his base on a personal level. His supporters saw him as a voice for the voiceless, someone who understood their struggles and refused to bow to the demands of political correctness. By standing firm on issues like religious freedom, economic revitalization, and national security, Trump demonstrated a commitment to his promises, even in the face of fierce resistance.

Navigating a Divided Nation

Trump inherited a deeply divided nation, but instead of shying away from the conflict, he confronted it head-on. His presidency was marked by bold decisions that polarized opinion but resonated deeply with those who shared his vision. From his strong stance on immigration to his efforts to renegotiate trade deals, Trump's actions reflected a willingness to lead decisively, regardless of the backlash.

Critics often accused Trump of exacerbating division, but his supporters saw his approach as necessary to challenge entrenched systems and ideologies. For them, his presidency was not about pleasing everyone—it was about standing firm in the truth, even when it was unpopular. This perspective echoed the biblical teaching that leaders must sometimes stand against the majority to fulfill God's purpose.

Faith as a Foundation for Resolve

Trump's resolve in the face of divisiveness was underpinned by his openness to faith and spiritual guidance. Throughout his presidency, Trump frequently engaged with faith leaders, participated in prayer events, and spoke of America's reliance on God. These actions were not just symbolic; they reflected his understanding of the spiritual dimensions of leadership.

For many Christians, Trump's ability to withstand relentless attacks was seen as evidence of divine favor. They believed that God was using him as an instrument to challenge societal decay and restore moral order. This belief gave Trump's supporters a sense of purpose, reinforcing their conviction that his leadership was part of a larger, God-ordained plan.

The Legacy of a Resolute Leader

Trump's presidency was not without controversy, but his determination to stand firm amidst divisiveness left an indelible mark on American history. His ability to navigate unprecedented opposition, while staying true to his principles, demonstrated a level of resolve that few leaders possess.

For his supporters, Trump's legacy is not defined by the chaos of his time in office but by his courage to confront it. They see him as a modern-day warrior, chosen to lead during a period of immense spiritual and political upheaval. His steadfastness, in the face of overwhelming odds, serves as a reminder that true leadership requires not just vision but the strength to endure the trials that come with it.

As this chapter explores Trump's journey through one of the most divisive eras in American politics, it becomes clear that his ability to stand firm was not just a political strategy—it was a calling. For those who believe in Trump's divine appointment, his resilience is proof that God equips His chosen leaders with the strength to persevere, even in the most challenging times.

THE EVANGELICAL EMBRACE

Donald J. Trump's rise to political prominence and his presidency sparked an unexpected alliance between an unconventional leader and a traditionally conservative religious base: evangelical Christians. Many observers initially doubted that the thrice-married billionaire, whose background was far removed from that of a typical churchgoer, could gain the enthusiastic support of America's most devout. Yet, not only did evangelicals rally behind Trump, but they became some of his staunchest defenders and most vocal advocates, viewing him as a divine instrument in a critical time of spiritual and cultural warfare.

This chapter explores the profound connection between Trump and the evangelical community, a relationship built on shared values, mutual respect, and a common mission to uphold America's Christian heritage. Trump's unapologetic defense of religious freedoms, his pro-life stance, and his commitment to restoring traditional values resonated deeply with millions of Christians who felt marginalized and ignored in an increasingly secular society.

While critics scoffed at the partnership, labeling it opportunistic or hypocritical, evangelicals saw something different. They perceived Trump as a Cyrus-like figure, a leader with flaws but chosen by God to advance His purposes. Just as the biblical King Cyrus was anointed to protect and restore God's people, Trump was seen as a protector of faith in a time when religious liberty seemed under attack.

This chapter delves into the reasons behind the evangelical embrace of Trump, examining the policies, promises, and symbolism that solidified his status as a champion of their cause. We will also address the criticisms leveled at this alliance and how evangelicals reconciled Trump's imperfections with their belief in his divine appointment.

The evangelical embrace of Trump was more than political—it was a spiritual alignment. For millions of believers, his presidency was a fulfillment of their prayers for a leader who would boldly defend their values and confront the forces seeking to undermine America's Judeo-Christian foundations. In this extraordinary alliance, Trump and the evangelical community formed a partnership that reshaped the political landscape and reaffirmed the enduring influence of faith in American life.

Why Christians Rally Behind Trump

Donald J. Trump's presidency marked a defining moment for America's evangelical Christians. Despite his unconventional background and personal flaws, millions of believers saw in him a leader uniquely positioned to champion their values, protect their freedoms, and confront the growing tide of secularism in society. For Christians across the nation, Trump was not merely a political ally but a divinely appointed figure whose boldness, policies, and rhetoric resonated deeply with their faith and mission.

This subchapter explores the reasons why Christians rallied so passionately behind Trump, highlighting the spiritual, cultural, and political dynamics that fueled their unwavering support.

A Defender of Religious Freedom

One of the primary reasons Christians rallied behind Trump was his steadfast commitment to religious liberty. For years, many believers felt their faith was under siege from secular forces intent on marginalizing religious expression. Trump's policies and executive orders reversed this trend, ensuring that Christians could freely practice and share their faith without fear of government interference.

His administration championed the rights of religious organizations, protected prayer in schools, and upheld the autonomy of faith-based institutions. Evangelical leaders lauded Trump as a president who not only listened to their concerns but acted decisively to address them. His defense of religious freedom was seen as a bulwark against the erosion of America's Christian heritage.

Aligning with Biblical Principles

Christians saw Trump's presidency as a beacon for

biblical values, especially in areas such as the sanctity of life, traditional marriage, and the protection of religious institutions. His pro-life stance, bolstered by significant policy decisions and judicial appointments, made him a hero to the millions who have prayed for an end to abortion.

Beyond policy, Trump's rhetoric often reflected a respect for America's Christian foundation. He spoke openly about the importance of faith, the power of prayer, and the need to honor God in public life. For Christians, these declarations were not just political talking points—they were affirmations of their core beliefs.

Fighting for the Forgotten

Christians were also drawn to Trump's populist message, which emphasized the needs of ordinary Americans over the interests of political elites. His promise to represent the "forgotten men and women" of the nation resonated deeply with believers who felt sidelined by cultural and political trends.

Trump's direct approach, often bypassing traditional media to communicate with his base, reinforced the perception that he was fighting for the people rather than the establishment. For many Christians, this populism mirrored biblical themes of standing up for the oppressed and challenging entrenched powers.

A Protector of Israel

Trump's unwavering support for Israel struck a chord with evangelical Christians, many of whom view the nation's fate as intertwined with biblical prophecy. His decision to recognize Jerusalem as the capital of Israel and relocate the U.S. Embassy there was celebrated as a historic and prophetic act.

Evangelicals saw Trump's Middle East policies, including the Abraham Accords, as further evidence of his alignment with God's plan. For a community deeply invested in the spiritual significance of Israel, Trump's actions reinforced their belief that his presidency was part of a divine narrative.

An Imperfect Vessel Chosen by God

Perhaps the most intriguing aspect of Trump's appeal to Christians is the way they reconciled his personal imperfections with their faith. To many evangelicals, Trump's flaws were not a disqualifier but rather evidence of God's ability to use imperfect people for His purposes.

Biblical figures like David, Paul, and even Moses were deeply flawed individuals who played pivotal roles in God's plan. Trump's brash personality, unorthodox methods, and past indiscretions were seen as irrelevant in light of the greater purpose they believed he was fulfilling. For millions of Christians, Trump's presidency was proof that God can raise up leaders from unexpected places to accomplish His will.

A Culture Warrior in a Time of Crisis

In an era marked by rapid cultural change, Trump's willingness to confront issues like political correctness, secularism, and moral relativism resonated strongly with Christians. He stood as a counterbalance to the progressive ideologies that many believers saw as a direct threat to their faith and values.

Trump's boldness in speaking out against these trends earned him a reputation as a "culture warrior." For Christians, his leadership was not about seeking consensus but about standing firm in the truth, even when it was unpopular. This courage endeared him to a community longing for a leader who would unapologetically defend their beliefs.

A Spiritual Awakening in Politics

Trump's presidency inspired a spiritual awakening within the political realm, as Christians mobilized to pray for the nation, advocate for their values, and support a leader they believed was chosen by God. His frequent engagements with faith leaders and public acknowledgments of prayer and divine guidance reinforced the perception that his administration was guided by a higher power.

For many, Trump's presidency was a reminder of the biblical promise in 2 Chronicles 7:14: "If my people, who are called by my name, will humble themselves and pray and seek my face and turn from their wicked ways, then I will hear from heaven, and I will forgive their sin and will heal their land." Evangelicals saw Trump as an answer to their prayers for a leader who would lead the nation back to its spiritual roots.

A Rallying Cry for the Faithful

The evangelical embrace of Trump was not merely a political alliance—it was a spiritual movement. Christians rallied behind him because they saw in his leadership a reflection of their deepest hopes and convictions. For them, Trump's presidency was a divine intervention, a moment when God used an unlikely leader to protect His people and restore righteousness to the nation.

As this subchapter illustrates, the Christian rallying cry for Trump was driven by a combination of faith, shared values, and a belief in his divine appointment. Whether defending religious liberty, championing biblical principles, or standing against cultural tides, Trump became a symbol of hope and resilience for millions of believers who saw in him a vessel of God's purpose.

The Role of Faith Leaders in His Rise

Donald Trump's ascent to the presidency was not merely a political phenomenon—it was a movement fueled by a deep partnership with America's faith leaders. From the earliest days of his campaign, Trump sought the counsel, support, and prayers of influential evangelical pastors and Christian leaders, recognizing their pivotal role in shaping public opinion and mobilizing millions of faithful voters. This partnership became a cornerstone of his rise, demonstrating the profound impact of faith in American politics.

Faith leaders played a multifaceted role in Trump's journey, serving as spiritual advisors, public advocates, and bridges between a candidate with an unconventional background and a deeply religious electorate. This subchapter explores how their involvement helped shape Trump's message, rally Christian support, and position him as a leader uniquely aligned with the values and vision of America's faith community.

Spiritual Advisors and Prayer Warriors

From the outset, Trump surrounded himself with a coalition of prominent faith leaders who provided him with spiritual guidance and prayerful support. Figures like Dr. James Dobson, Pastor Robert Jeffress, and Rev. Franklin Graham became integral to his campaign, offering advice on issues important to evangelicals and reassuring believers of Trump's commitment to their values.

Trump's decision to establish a "faith advisory council" was unprecedented, signaling his intent to place the concerns of Christians at the heart of his presidency. These advisors not only prayed with and for Trump but also shared their confidence that he was God's chosen instrument for a critical time in America's history.

Advocates for Trump's Candidacy

Faith leaders also played a vital role in publicly endorsing Trump and addressing concerns about his past. In rallies, sermons, and media appearances, these leaders explained why they believed Trump's policies, promises, and courage outweighed any personal imperfections.

Leaders like Jerry Falwell Jr., Paula White-Cain, and Pastor Mark Burns emerged as some of Trump's most vocal supporters. They emphasized his commitment to religious liberty, his pro-life stance, and his defense of Israel—key issues for evangelicals. Their endorsements carried significant weight, persuading many Christians to view Trump not through the lens of his flaws but as a "modern-day Cyrus" chosen by God to lead the nation.

Mobilizing the Faithful

The involvement of faith leaders was instrumental in mobilizing evangelical voters, who constituted a critical bloc in Trump's electoral victory. Churches became hubs for voter registration drives and prayer meetings, while sermons often emphasized the importance of participating in the democratic process as an act of faith.

Faith leaders used their platforms to rally Christians to vote for a candidate who would defend their freedoms and uphold biblical principles. The result was an unprecedented turnout of evangelical voters, with over 80% of white evangelicals casting their ballots for Trump in 2016—a decisive factor in his victory.

Shaping the Narrative

Faith leaders helped shape the narrative of Trump's candidacy as part of a divine plan. Drawing parallels to biblical figures like King David and the Apostle Paul, they framed Trump as an imperfect vessel chosen by God to lead the nation through turbulent times.

This messaging resonated deeply with believers who saw their own struggles and imperfections reflected in Trump's journey. It also reframed his past missteps as evidence of God's transformative power, reinforcing the idea that Trump's presidency was part of a greater spiritual narrative.

Champions of Religious Liberty

Faith leaders were not only advocates for Trump but also defenders of his policies once in office. They praised his executive orders protecting religious freedom, his efforts to appoint conservative judges, and his pro-life agenda. These leaders became conduits for communicating Trump's accomplishments to their congregations, ensuring that his presidency remained closely aligned with the priorities of the evangelical community.

A Symbiotic Partnership

The relationship between Trump and America's faith leaders was mutually beneficial. For Trump, their support provided moral credibility and a direct connection to millions of voters. For faith leaders, his presidency offered an unprecedented opportunity to influence national policy and restore the prominence of Christian values in public life.

This partnership was not without its critics, who questioned the alignment of faith with politics. However, for millions of Christians, the collaboration between Trump and their spiritual leaders was a testament to God's hand at work in the nation's highest office.

A Legacy of Faith-Driven Leadership

The role of faith leaders in Trump's rise cannot be overstated. They were more than supporters—they were architects of a movement that brought faith to the forefront of American politics. Their prayers, endorsements, and advocacy helped solidify Trump's position as a leader uniquely attuned to the needs and aspirations of the evangelical community.

For millions of believers, the involvement of faith leaders was further confirmation that Trump's presidency was not a political accident but a divine appointment. By standing alongside him, these leaders reinforced the belief that God had raised up Donald Trump for such a time as this, uniting faith and leadership in a shared mission to restore America's Christian heritage.

SPIRITUAL WARFARE

Donald Trump's presidency was not merely a political event; it was a spiritual battleground that exposed the deeper, unseen forces at work in America's cultural and political landscape. To his supporters, Trump's time in office was a testament to the ongoing conflict between good and evil, light and darkness. His leadership became a focal point in the larger narrative of spiritual warfare, a cosmic struggle that has shaped nations and guided the course of human history.

This chapter delves into the spiritual undercurrents of Trump's presidency, exploring how his rise to power was met with fierce opposition that often seemed to transcend the natural realm. From the unprecedented hostility he faced in the media to the coordinated efforts to undermine his policies, many of his supporters interpreted these events as evidence of a larger, more sinister agenda aimed at silencing truth and erasing faith from the public square.

The Unseen Battle

Ephesians 6:12 reminds believers, "For we do not wrestle against flesh and blood, but against the rulers, against the authorities, against the cosmic powers over this present darkness, against the spiritual forces of evil in the heavenly places." For many Christians, this verse encapsulated the reality of Trump's presidency. They viewed the relentless attacks on his character, policies, and supporters as manifestations of this spiritual struggle—a clash between forces determined to uphold biblical values and those intent on their destruction.

Trump's bold stances on issues like religious liberty, the sanctity of life, and support for Israel made him a target not only in the political arena but also in the spiritual one. His presidency was marked by moments that many saw as divine victories, such as the Supreme Court appointments that upheld conservative principles and the historic recognition of Jerusalem as Israel's capital. Yet, these triumphs were often met with equally intense resistance, further solidifying the perception that Trump's leadership was at the center of a spiritual conflict.

A Divisive Figure in a Divided World

The polarization surrounding Trump was unlike anything seen in modern American history. To his supporters, he was a protector of faith and freedom, a man chosen by God to lead the nation back to its spiritual foundations. To his detractors, he was a disruptor, a symbol of everything they opposed. This stark division was not merely political—it was deeply spiritual, reflecting the broader moral and ethical battles that have defined America's cultural trajectory.

Faith leaders and prayer warriors recognized the need to intercede on Trump's behalf, believing that his leadership represented a critical juncture in the nation's destiny. Prayer rallies, fasting initiatives, and calls for spiritual awakening became commonplace during his presidency, as millions of Christians sought divine intervention in what they perceived as a battle for America's soul.

Trump as a Spiritual Warrior

While Trump himself rarely framed his presidency in explicitly spiritual terms, his actions often aligned with the values and priorities of America's faith community. His willingness to confront political correctness, champion conservative principles, and challenge entrenched institutions resonated deeply with believers who saw in him a leader willing to fight for their beliefs.

To his supporters, Trump's brash personality and unorthodox methods were not flaws but necessary traits for a leader engaged in spiritual warfare. Just as biblical figures like Joshua and Gideon were called to lead in times of conflict, Trump's boldness was seen as a divine asset in the face of unprecedented challenges.

The Role of the Church

The Church played a pivotal role in this spiritual struggle, rallying around Trump as a beacon of hope and resilience. Faith leaders frequently spoke of the need for unity, prayer, and action, urging believers to stand firm in the face of opposition. For many Christians, supporting Trump was not just a political choice but a spiritual mandate, a way to affirm their commitment to God's plan for America.

As we delve deeper into this chapter, we will examine the key moments that defined Trump's presidency as a period of spiritual warfare. From the cultural clashes over morality and religious freedom to the prophetic voices that rallied the faithful, this chapter uncovers the spiritual dimensions of a presidency that forever changed the landscape of American politics and faith.

Trump's story is not just one of political triumphs and challenges—it is a testament to the power of faith in the face of adversity and the enduring truth that, in the midst of the fiercest battles, God's hand remains steadfastly at work.

Trump's Presidency in the Battle of Good vs. Evil

Donald Trump's presidency was more than a political phenomenon; it was a defining moment in a spiritual battle that had been brewing for decades. For many of his supporters, his rise to power represented the beginning of a fight to reclaim America's moral and spiritual identity. Trump was not merely a leader but a warrior standing on the front lines of a conflict between good and evil, truth and deception, light and darkness.

The Unmistakable Signs of a Spiritual Battle

From the moment Trump announced his candidacy, the opposition he faced was swift, relentless, and unprecedented. Critics attacked not only his policies but also his character, his family, and even his faith. To millions of believers, this level of vitriol was no coincidence—it was evidence of a spiritual battle being waged against a man chosen to disrupt the status quo and champion God's principles.

Faith leaders and their congregations identified clear signs of this conflict. The media's bias, widespread misinformation, and coordinated efforts to undermine Trump's presidency were viewed as tools of an adversarial force intent on dismantling the Judeo-Christian foundations of the nation. They saw Trump as a David-like figure, standing up to a modern-day Goliath of cultural, political, and spiritual opposition.

Policies That Sparked a Moral Revival

Trump's presidency was marked by bold decisions that rallied believers and advanced causes deeply rooted in Christian values. His unwavering pro-life stance, which led to significant victories in the fight against abortion, was celebrated as a triumph for those who saw the sanctity of life as a cornerstone of their faith. Similarly, his defense of religious freedoms, including protections for churches and faith-based organizations, was seen as a direct blow to the forces seeking to marginalize Christianity in public life.

The decision to recognize Jerusalem as Israel's capital and relocate the U.S. embassy was another key moment. For Christians, this move carried profound spiritual significance, aligning with biblical prophecy and reaffirming America's role as a protector of God's chosen people. To his supporters, these actions demonstrated Trump's willingness to align his presidency with God's will, even in the face of fierce global criticism.

The Opposition as a Manifestation of Darkness

Throughout Trump's presidency, his detractors became increasingly vocal and aggressive, sparking a level of division and animosity rarely seen in American politics. Many Christians interpreted this opposition as a manifestation of deeper spiritual forces seeking to thwart God's plan. They pointed to efforts to impeach Trump, the relentless criticism from mainstream media, and the cultural pushback against his policies as evidence of a coordinated attack on truth and righteousness.

This conflict extended beyond the political arena into cultural and moral debates. Issues like gender identity, religious expression, and the sanctity of marriage became flashpoints in the broader spiritual battle. Trump's boldness in addressing these topics made him a target, but it also solidified his role as a defender of traditional values.

The Role of Prayer in the Fight

Recognizing the spiritual nature of this battle, millions of Christians turned to prayer as a weapon of choice. Prayer rallies, intercession campaigns, and fasting initiatives became hallmarks of Trump's presidency, as believers sought divine protection and guidance for their leader. Faith leaders across the country called on their congregations to engage in spiritual warfare, praying for Trump's strength, wisdom, and success in fulfilling his God-given mission.

For many, the prayers were answered in moments of unexpected triumph, such as the confirmation of conservative Supreme Court justices and the robust defense of religious freedoms. These victories were seen not only as political achievements but as spiritual breakthroughs, further affirming the belief that Trump's presidency was divinely ordained.

Trump as a Beacon of Hope in a Time of Conflict

To his supporters, Trump's willingness to confront the cultural and political establishment was a reflection of his divine purpose. His unyielding stance on issues of faith and morality inspired millions, offering hope that the battle against darkness could be won. While his presidency was not without controversy, his actions consistently aligned with the values of those who saw him as a vessel for God's work.

This spiritual battle was not merely about Donald Trump as an individual but about the larger mission he represented—a call to restore America's spiritual foundation, defend biblical truth, and stand firm against the encroaching forces of secularism and moral decay.

A Legacy of Spiritual Resistance

As the chapter unfolds, we will explore the ways in which Trump's presidency became a rallying point for believers engaged in spiritual warfare. His leadership, though unconventional, was a testament to the enduring power of faith in the face of opposition. For millions of Christians, Trump was more than a political leader—he was a symbol of hope, resilience, and divine purpose in a time of great uncertainty.

Ultimately, Trump's presidency will be remembered not just for its policies or achievements but for the spiritual awakening it inspired. In the battle between good and evil, his leadership stood as a beacon of light, reminding believers that even in the darkest times, God's hand remains at work.

The Power of Prayer in Politics

Prayer has long been a cornerstone of America's identity, shaping its leaders, policies, and cultural trajectory. But during Donald Trump's presidency, the power of prayer emerged in an unprecedented way, becoming a unifying force for millions who believed they were fighting a spiritual battle for the nation's soul. Trump's leadership not only inspired widespread prayer movements but also highlighted the profound impact of faith in guiding political decisions and sustaining leaders through extraordinary challenges.

Trump's Embrace of Prayer

Donald Trump's presidency was characterized by a bold acknowledgment of the role faith plays in governance and public life. From the earliest days of his campaign, Trump sought the counsel and support of prominent Christian leaders, recognizing the value of spiritual wisdom in navigating the turbulent waters of politics. His willingness to openly embrace prayer—whether during public rallies, private meetings, or in the Oval Office—set him apart as a leader unafraid to acknowledge his dependence on divine guidance.

Images of Trump bowing his head as faith leaders laid hands on him became iconic symbols of his presidency. These moments resonated deeply with millions of Americans who saw them as evidence of his humility before God and his commitment to seeking divine wisdom in leading the nation. In Trump, they saw a leader willing to fight for religious freedom and uphold biblical principles, even as he faced relentless opposition.

A Nationwide Prayer Movement

Under Trump's leadership, prayer became a rallying cry for millions of Christians who believed the nation was at a crossroads. Recognizing the spiritual nature of the challenges facing America, believers across the country organized prayer rallies, fasting campaigns, and intercessory networks to support their president and seek divine intervention.

These prayer movements transcended denominational lines, uniting believers in a shared mission to uphold God's will for the nation. Events like Franklin Graham's Decision America Tour and the annual National Day of Prayer saw record participation during Trump's presidency, as faith leaders urged their congregations to pray for the president, his administration, and the nation's future.

Trump's supporters believed that these collective prayers had tangible results, pointing to significant victories during his presidency. The confirmation of conservative Supreme Court justices, the defense of religious freedoms, and landmark decisions on issues like pro-life policies were seen as answers to prayer and evidence of God's favor on Trump's administration.

Prayer as a Weapon in Spiritual Warfare

For many Christians, prayer was more than a spiritual discipline—it was a weapon in the ongoing battle between good and evil. They viewed Trump's presidency as a direct challenge to forces seeking to undermine America's Christian heritage and moral foundations. Prayer became a way to counteract the opposition he faced, from hostile media narratives to political gridlock and cultural polarization.

Scripture underscores the power of prayer in spiritual warfare, with verses like 2 Chronicles 7:14 offering a roadmap for national renewal: "If my people, who are called by my name, will humble themselves and pray and seek my face and turn from their wicked ways, then I will hear from heaven, and I will forgive their sin and will heal their land." Trump's presidency inspired countless believers to act on this promise, interceding for their leader and the nation with renewed fervor.

Trump's Impact on Faith Leaders

Trump's presidency also had a profound impact on

faith leaders, many of whom stepped into the political arena more boldly than ever before. Figures like Paula White, Franklin Graham, and Robert Jeffress became prominent voices advocating for prayer and supporting Trump as a God-ordained leader. These leaders often spoke of the spiritual warfare surrounding Trump's presidency, urging their followers to stand firm in faith and continue praying for divine protection and guidance.

Trump's openness to faith leaders and their prayers reinforced his image as a president aligned with God's purposes. By inviting pastors and spiritual advisors into the White House and seeking their counsel on key issues, he demonstrated a commitment to grounding his leadership in biblical principles—a stark contrast to the secularism often seen in modern politics.

A Legacy of Prayer-Driven Leadership

The legacy of Trump's presidency extends far beyond policy achievements; it represents a revival of prayer-driven leadership in American politics. For millions of Christians, his time in office was a reminder of the power of prayer to influence nations and change the course of history. They saw Trump not just as a president but as a vessel through whom God could work to restore righteousness, protect religious freedoms, and uphold biblical values.

As this chapter explores, the role of prayer in Trump's presidency serves as a testament to the enduring power of faith in the political sphere. It underscores the truth that, in times of uncertainty and division, prayer remains a vital force for unity, strength, and divine intervention. For those who believe in Trump's divine appointment, the power of prayer was not just a background element but a driving force in his rise, his victories, and his enduring influence on the nation.

In Trump's presidency, the faithful found renewed hope that, through prayer, even the most daunting challenges could be overcome and that America's destiny as a nation under God could be reclaimed.

LEGACY AND THE FUTURE

Donald J. Trump's presidency was nothing short of transformative. His time in office disrupted the political establishment, reignited the cultural conversation on faith, and left an indelible mark on the global stage. To his supporters, Trump was more than a leader—he was a movement, a symbol of hope, and a force for moral and spiritual revival. As the world continues to grapple with his legacy, one question remains: what does the future hold for a nation shaped by his influence?

Trump's presidency broke conventional molds and set a new standard for leadership that prioritized action over rhetoric, principles over politics, and results over popularity. While his detractors worked tirelessly to diminish his accomplishments, the undeniable impact of his policies and persona continues to ripple across America and the world. For those who see his rise as divinely orchestrated, his legacy is a testament to God's ability to work through unconventional vessels to achieve extraordinary outcomes.

A Presidency of Unparalleled Impact

Trump's administration was marked by a series of historic achievements that resonated deeply with his supporters, particularly within the Christian community. From appointing conservative judges who reshaped the judiciary to defending religious liberties and supporting pro-life initiatives, Trump's policies were seen as direct answers to prayer and evidence of

God's hand at work.

Beyond policy, Trump's bold and unapologetic leadership style inspired millions who felt marginalized or silenced by the growing tide of political correctness. To his followers, he was a modern-day warrior, unafraid to confront cultural decay and restore the foundational values that once made America a beacon of hope and freedom.

A Legacy Written in Faith and Action

Trump's presidency also ushered in a spiritual awakening for many Americans. Prayer movements, intercessory gatherings, and a renewed focus on biblical principles became hallmarks of his time in office. Evangelical leaders and grassroots organizations rallied behind his vision, recognizing in him a leader willing to align the nation's future with God's purposes.

For millions of believers, Trump's legacy is not confined to his time in the White House. It is a call to action, a reminder that faith and courage can reshape a nation's destiny. His presidency challenged Christians to rise above complacency and engage in the spiritual and cultural battles that define our time.

The Path Forward

As this chapter will explore, Trump's legacy is not simply a reflection of his past accomplishments but a roadmap for the future. It invites believers to consider how they can carry forward the torch of faith, freedom, and righteousness that his presidency ignited.

For those who see Trump as a God-appointed leader, his time in office was only the beginning. Whether through his continued influence in politics, the rise of leaders inspired by his example, or the lasting impact of his policies, the Trump era has set the stage for a new chapter in America's story.

Ultimately, the legacy of Donald Trump transcends politics. It is a story of divine purpose, relentless determination, and unwavering faith in the face of opposition. As we delve into his enduring influence and the path ahead, we are reminded that God's plans often unfold through unexpected leaders and extraordinary circumstances.

The future remains unwritten, but one thing is clear: the movement Trump began continues to shape hearts, minds, and destinies. His legacy is not just a reflection of what was but a promise of what could be—a brighter, freer, and more faithful America grounded in the timeless truths of God's Word.

Examining the Impact of His Presidency

The presidency of Donald J. Trump was a seismic event in American politics and culture. His leadership reshaped the nation, redefining what it means to lead with boldness, conviction, and an unapologetic commitment to principle. While critics sought to undermine his achievements, the undeniable impact of Trump's presidency continues to resonate with millions of Americans and beyond, leaving a legacy that many consider not only transformative but divinely inspired.

Rebuilding America's Foundations

Trump's presidency was marked by a commitment to restoring the principles that made America a global leader. His "America First" agenda revitalized the economy, prioritized national security, and reinstilled a sense of pride in the nation's identity. Policies such as tax cuts, deregulation, and renegotiation of trade agreements spurred unprecedented economic growth, while record-low unemployment for minority groups showcased his administration's focus on uplifting all Americans.

For Christians, Trump's presidency stood as a bulwark against the encroachment of secularism. His defense of religious liberties, both domestically and internationally, was hailed as a victory for believers worldwide. The establishment of the White House Faith and Opportunity Initiative symbolized his commitment to fostering a culture that respected and protected the role of faith in public life.

Judicial Appointments: A Lasting Legacy

Perhaps one of the most enduring aspects of Trump's presidency is his reshaping of the federal judiciary. His appointment of three conservative Supreme Court justices—Neil Gorsuch, Brett Kavanaugh, and Amy Coney Barrett—shifted the balance of the court for a generation. These appointments paved the way for significant rulings, including the overturning of Roe v. Wade, a landmark decision that reinvigorated the pro-life movement and underscored the importance of judicial conservatism.

In addition to the Supreme Court, Trump appointed more than 200 federal judges, ensuring a legacy of constitutional interpretation grounded in originalist principles. This judicial shift was celebrated by his supporters as a divine intervention to restore justice and righteousness to the nation's legal system.

The Cultural Awakening

Trump's presidency was not just a political movement—it was a cultural awakening. His bold rhetoric and willingness to challenge political correctness emboldened millions of Americans who felt silenced by the progressive elite. He became a champion for those who believed that traditional values were under siege, inspiring grassroots movements across the nation to rise up and reclaim their voice.

The cultural impact of his presidency extended to the global stage, where Trump reasserted America's position as a leader in defending freedom and faith. His unwavering support for Israel, including the historic recognition of Jerusalem as its capital, was celebrated by Christians worldwide as a fulfillment of biblical prophecy. These actions reinforced his image as a leader aligned with God's purposes, unafraid to make bold decisions in the face of opposition.

Uniting Believers in a Common Mission

While Trump's presidency was divisive for the nation, it united Christians in an unprecedented way. Prayer movements, intercessory campaigns, and faith-based initiatives flourished during his time in office, as believers rallied behind a leader they saw as God-appointed. Events like the Evangelicals for Trump coalition highlighted the deep connection between his presidency and the Christian community, cementing his role as a spiritual as well as political figure.

A Legacy Beyond the White House

The impact of Trump's presidency extends far beyond his four years in office. His policies and leadership style have inspired a new generation of leaders to embrace boldness and faith in the political arena. His commitment to religious freedom, pro-life values, and America's sovereignty set a precedent for future administrations to follow, ensuring that his legacy will endure in the years to come.

For millions of believers, Trump's presidency was a reminder that God often works through unconventional leaders to accomplish His purposes. His time in office demonstrated that even in the face of relentless opposition, a leader guided by conviction and faith can leave a lasting impact on a nation and the world.

As we examine the impact of Trump's presidency, it becomes clear that his legacy is not just a chapter in America's history but a testament to the power of divine purpose in shaping the course of nations. Whether through his policies, his cultural influence, or his unwavering commitment to faith, Trump's presidency continues to inspire millions to stand firm in their beliefs and work toward a future that aligns with God's vision for America.

What Lies Ahead for God's Appointee

As the era of Donald J. Trump's presidency continues to be analyzed and celebrated by his supporters, one question dominates the minds of millions: what lies ahead for a leader many believe was appointed by God? Is his mission complete, or is there more to come? While history has yet to fully unveil its answers, the signs suggest that Trump's role on the stage of divine destiny is far from over.

A Movement, Not a Moment

Trump's influence transcends his time in office. From his first campaign in 2016 to his ongoing presence as a cultural and political icon, Trump has built a movement that stands as a bulwark against the forces of secularism, globalism, and moral decline. This movement, rooted in faith, patriotism, and an unwavering belief in America's greatness, continues to gain momentum, inspiring millions to remain vigilant in defending their values.

The rise of Trump-endorsed candidates, his continued influence on the Republican Party, and his unyielding presence in the media point to a leader who is not stepping aside but preparing for the next chapter. Whether through a return to public office or as a guiding force for future leaders, Trump's influence remains a cornerstone of American politics.

The Second Term

For many of Trump's supporters, the second term is not just a political aspiration — it is a spiritual imperative. They view his unfinished work as a call to action, a divine mandate to continue the fight for religious freedom, judicial conservatism, and national sovereignty. The controversies surrounding the 2020 election have only solidified their belief that Trump's mission is far from complete.

A second Trump presidency, they argue, will allow him to build upon the foundations he laid during his first term. From strengthening the judiciary to combating cultural decay, his return to the White House would be seen as a continuation of God's plan for America.

A Role Beyond the Presidency

Even if Trump does not return to the Oval Office, his role as a spiritual and political leader remains undeniable. As the de facto head of a movement that prioritizes faith and freedom, Trump has the potential to influence future leaders, mentor emerging voices, and shape the direction of the Republican Party for years to come.

Moreover, Trump's presence on the global stage has solidified his reputation as a defender of Christian values and a staunch ally of Israel. His continued advocacy for these causes ensures that his influence will extend beyond America's borders, inspiring believers worldwide to stand firm in their convictions.

The Unfolding of God's Plan

For those who see Trump as God's appointee, his journey is a testament to the unpredictable and often surprising ways in which God works through His chosen leaders. Trump's rise to power, his presidency, and his ongoing influence all point to a larger narrative—one that is not yet complete.

The trials and triumphs he has faced serve as a reminder that God's purposes often involve periods of testing and perseverance. Just as biblical figures like Joseph and David faced challenges before fulfilling their destinies, Trump's path may also include obstacles that refine his character and strengthen his resolve.

A Call to Action

As we consider what lies ahead for Donald Trump, it is clear that his supporters have a crucial role to play. Through prayer, advocacy, and active participation in the political process, they can help ensure that the values Trump championed continue to shape the nation's future.

Whether as a candidate, a kingmaker, or a cultural icon, Trump's mission reflects a broader spiritual battle for the soul of America. His supporters believe that by standing with him, they are standing for God's vision for the nation—a vision of freedom, faith, and righteousness.

A Future Full of Promise

Ultimately, the question of what lies ahead for Donald Trump is one that only time—and God—can answer. Yet, the evidence suggests that his role as a leader and a symbol of divine purpose is far from over. Whether through his direct actions or the enduring impact of his movement, Trump's influence will continue to shape the political and spiritual landscape for years to come.

As we close this chapter, we are reminded that God's appointees often work in ways that defy human expectations. Trump's story is still being written, and for those who believe in his divine calling, the best is yet to come.

CONCLUSION: REFLECTION ON FAITH AND LEADERSHIP

Donald J. Trump's journey from businessman to the 45th President of the United States is more than a remarkable political story—it is a testament to the enduring power of faith and leadership in shaping history. For millions of Americans, Trump embodies the belief that God works through chosen individuals, even those who may seem unconventional or unorthodox, to achieve His purposes. His presidency, filled with bold decisions and relentless perseverance, invites us to reflect on the profound connection between divine providence and human leadership.

The Legacy of an Unconventional Leader

Trump's leadership style was unlike any other seen in modern American politics. Direct, unapologetic, and driven by conviction, he broke through the barriers of political correctness and challenged the status quo. For his supporters, these traits were not just political strategies—they were signs of a leader guided by a higher purpose. His unwavering defense of religious liberties, his commitment to Israel, and his pro-life advocacy resonated deeply with people of faith who saw his actions as aligning with biblical values.

Even in the face of relentless opposition, Trump remained steadfast, demonstrating the kind of resolve that echoes the trials faced by biblical figures. Like Joseph, who endured betrayal, and David, who faced giants, Trump navigated a political landscape fraught with challenges, emerging as a symbol of resilience and divine favor.

Faith as the Foundation

At the heart of Trump's presidency was a profound recognition of the role of faith in American society. His policies and rhetoric consistently emphasized the importance of religious freedom and the preservation of traditional values. For many Christians, his leadership was a reminder that faith is not just a private matter but a guiding force for public life.

Through his actions, Trump reignited conversations about the role of God in governance, inspiring believers to engage more actively in the political process. His presidency became a rallying point for prayer movements and faith-based initiatives, illustrating the power of collective spiritual action in shaping a nation's destiny.

A Call to Future Leaders

Trump's presidency also serves as a blueprint for future leaders who seek to integrate faith with governance. His boldness, coupled with his willingness to champion causes aligned with Christian principles, demonstrated that it is possible to lead with conviction even in a polarized world. For those who believe in his divine appointment, Trump's time in office was not just about policy—it was about fulfilling a God-ordained mission to restore righteousness and accountability to the highest levels of power.

The Role of Believers Moving Forward

As we look to the future, Trump's legacy challenges believers to remain vigilant and active in their faith. His presidency underscored the importance of prayer, community, and unwavering commitment to God's purposes. Whether through political advocacy, supporting faith-based initiatives, or simply standing firm in their convictions, Trump's supporters are called to continue the work he began.

The story of Donald Trump's leadership reminds us that God often chooses the most unexpected individuals to carry out His plans. His presidency was a moment of divine disruption, shaking the foundations of a complacent political system and inspiring millions to reexamine their own roles in God's greater plan.

A Legacy of Faith and Boldness

In reflecting on Trump's leadership, we are reminded of the power of faith to guide even the most unconventional leaders. His presidency stands as a testament to the belief that God can use anyone—flaws and all—to achieve extraordinary things. For millions of Americans and countless others worldwide, Trump's time in office was a beacon of hope, courage, and divine purpose.

As the chapter of Trump's presidency transitions to the next phase of his journey, his legacy endures as a call to action for those who believe in the transformative power of faith and leadership. Whether seen as a disruptor, a defender, or a divinely chosen leader, Donald J. Trump remains a figure whose impact will be felt for generations to come.